Naming the Island

Judith Neeld

For Judith Steinburgh
"this is the way
we mend our lives"

Judith Neeld

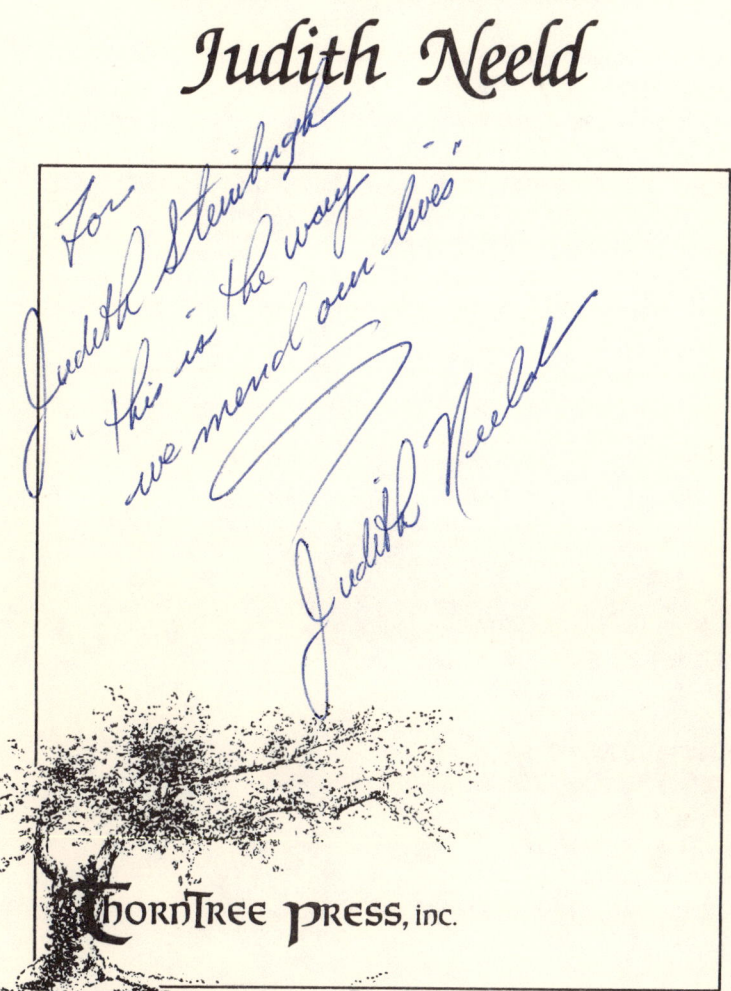

ThornTree Press, inc.

Copyright c 1988 by Judith Neeld
All rights reserved
Printed in the United States of America
First Edition
First Printing

A number of these poems, some in different versions, appear in the following publications. Grateful acknowledgement is made to:

Black Willow; Brooklyn Review; Calyx; Colorado Review; Creeping Bent; Crosscurrents, A Quarterly; Crow Dancing; Descant; Embers; Hampden-Sydney Poetry Review; Journal of New Jersey Poets; Massachusetts Review; Menominie Review; Mid-American Review; Nycticorax; Osiris; Phoebe; Poets On; St. Andrews Review; Sandscript; Southwest Review; Tar River Poetry; The Cape Rock; The Denny Prize Poems Anthology, 1982 and 1983; The Greenfield Review; The Old Red Kimono; The Poetry Review; The Texas Review; Yarrow.

"Ornithology in November" appeared as the 1985 Andrew Mountain Press Prize Pamphlet.

By the same author: SEA FIRE, a chapbook (Adastra Press, 1987)
　　　　　　　　　　　SCRIPTS FOR A LIFE IN THREE PARTS (Stone Country Press, 1978)

Cover art by Pat McCormick
Book design by Peggy Shearn
Logo by Laura M. Doyle

ISBN: 0-939395-08-8
Library of Congress Catalog Number: 88-5029

Published in 1988 by
Thorntree Press, Inc.
547 Hawthorn Lane, Winnetka, IL 60093

CONTENTS

I Hunters And Lovers

- 6 Hawk
- 7 Bee - A Still Life
- 8 Leaving The Cats
- 9 First Year Of The Vine
- 10 Hunters And Lovers
- 11 Variation On A Theme Of Incest
- 12 Without Looking Back Or Understanding
- 13 Of Six Young Tomato Plants
- 14 Mourning Before The Fact
- 15 The Boy And The Catch
- 16 Hurricane Over A Country Bordering On The Gulf Of Mexico
- 17 Two Windows Of The Cathedral
- 19 Monet's Garden: In Camera
- 20 The Last Summer In Llanberis
- 22 Ornithology In November
- 24 Christmas Bird Count

II Homecoming Of The North Coast Wife

- 26 Farm Wife At Harvest
- 27 Her Topography
- 28 Where The Barn Leans Empty
- 29 Homecoming Of The North Coast Wife
- 30 The Day Color Warped From Our Sister's Eyes
- 31 A Discrete Flowering
- 32 First Son
- 33 The Christening Of The Monogoloid Child
- 34 When They Pull You From My River, Caroling

35 The Caretakers:
   Closing For The Season
36 Three Poems At The Fall Equinox
37 Over Dartmoor: The Climb At Hound Tor
38 J. Calvin's Daughter
39 Motion Counterclockwise
40 Ground-Hog Day
41 To A House On The Market

III Falling Into The Dream

43 Summer Island
44 In The Mid-Island
46 Exhibition In Rain
47 April Fool's Day
48 Beachcombing in Skein Cove
49 Notes For Swimming Or Dancing
   After A Lunar Eclipse
50 Flocking
51 When The Sea Bird Has Gone: Concert
52 Poem For The Summer
53 Letters From The Islands
55 Sea Fire
56 Writing The Ocean After A Storm
57 October
58 Two Who Died Before Winter
59 Falling Into The Dream
60 Flood: The Island Becomes Water
61 The House Of Receiving
63 Naming The Island
64 The Warming Of A Glass House

I

HUNTERS AND LOVERS

*for
R.H.N.*

*"...time burrowing in'
ledge over ledge, dovetailing,
holding on."*
　　　—Brendan Galvin

HAWK

Up there she plays on the wind, rolling
like a favorite note
from tongue to heart; at the flute end
she is a song
strung across the compassionate
letters of rain.
Another day, and
the bird will peel into a sky
of contours absolute as its bones
to work a killer's odds on
sisters
in the broken hollows of the air.

Downwind a thousand times, one
second before earth this time
cursed by a feather cast
the approach misjudged:
the dragged wing, the doomed leg
become
all that remain of her life.

But more's at stake.
A death dropping to land:
and that
other precise moment
the ecstacy
of home.

BEE - A STILL LIFE

The poem's lost, my hands' page
unmessaged again. Your legs
did it: so thick with rose sludge you had to
put down, made me weigh language

like pollen. We're the wrong sort
to book it together. I ought
to have thrown you out, landing, but thought my words
and your job were the same door;

should have dissected your wings, seen
how each line is rhymed sweeter
than syllables — cleaner, won't cry the dark
like the lightning in my sleep.

In this blood I wear, there's some-
thing sting could turn to poison.
I can kill you now, Cousin, and never
learn which of us has won.

LEAVING THE CATS

A door closes.
You fall on the window garden
stenciling its loose earth
like a soiled snow, then
stretch out soft, languid

with anger. I know your loss
the grief of a presence suddenly gone —
though the signs you could have read
were there:
the water bowls topped off
the box retrenched
the food put down
to a purpose too close. Then

I am the one who comes after
this home is destroyed by your love;
to sweep the rug
ease a stem
paint scratches clean from tables
and flesh. My saints

I would teach you absence as blessing.

FIRST YEAR OF THE VINE

    1.
Winter, and the terrible patience
of her seed
when nothing grows.

    2.
Then, too little time:
she goes from leaf to flower
to fruit
the cartography of ruin
trolling
each indescribable step.

    3.
Stem and roots clawing
raw
and the damned
sun straddles her bed.

    4.
After it
this earth wrinkle's shingled
in green.
No one said: *hold on.*
Hold on or die.
The line is straight enough
from hunger up.

HUNTERS AND LOVERS

A cat enters the yard.

She waits
for the sign.
She is artist
philosopher
critic: the charwoman
cleaning nightsoil from her feet.
Shade festers on mid-summer's back.
The sparrows freeze.
This girl is an old daughter
of a game and
I cast the first stones.
She usurps a tree
is dethroned.
Without this prize
the birds would die today.

Now, as I write
to you in the stalk of love
a branch falls:
a rib
a broken wing.
Our trap.
Our sign.

VARIATION ON A THEME OF INCEST

Where the ground shrugs off
into the old brown river
you choose a place
for its layers of sod—
read from my page, then yours.
We may be next
of kin
cross-legged, without blankets
the liquor between us.
I believe first
impressions and am too simple.

Black Irish, by your own account
and working enough to get on, move often—
left your last woman
in Phillipsburg—came here
to oblige the clan's barn raising and hogs.

Sweating August, I came down
a highway, dodging trucks, missed
the first turn
turned around, gambled
on landmarks. Left behind orders
combining the stepchildren and love.

Shirts cling to our backs like oil and wine.
It is too hot for a good thirst.
When the books no longer work—blood
brother, I learn
how water that looks careless
claws back and cuts
an island
out of the unwitting earth.

WITHOUT LOOKING BACK OR UNDERSTANDING

The blue lines crowd and break
beach grass is seen as arrows
quivered and on guard.
Our voices move like the end and
the beginning of a tide:
slowly at first, then taking a direction
something beyond us claims.
It is a hard quarrel to leave undone.

On days like this
I am steeled to an element
cold as the blue farthings of your eyes
when the water ebbs between us.
Not good at defaults
I take the latest wave shoulder on
while you hold
for the slow cooling
the coming of flesh to its equal sea.

There are other mornings
when a brown mist opens across
the cut where brown draggers head
out, purposed, and jowled
down: somehow
we have slept the night together.

It is no one's fault.
A symptom of hurricane: the ache
between pores
the nerve ends of the sea
these passings, one
condition becoming the next.

OF SIX YOUNG TOMATO PLANTS

One will live brilliantly
because the trowel stroked clean.
Another has broken short: root-shocked
its stem fights the sun alone.

And the nights will freeze.
There have been a few inches of rain.
How the rest grow is not
a matter of race or sex.

They are dancers reeling in the wind
through its cold squares: they are hands
undefended from frost, where the first joint rots.
How we have gotten the small deaths by heart!

But now and then a new bud nails itself
to the ruined flesh. This is the way
we mend our lives: by harvest
the spring scars will be redressed.

MOURNING BEFORE THE FACT

Sun bends through the windows—this day
ages and the house sheds
paint like leaves of the diseased
and helpless elm; I bend
to a fire that mirrors me
in these separations you leave
behind, and in it, see
the head breaking through glass
to its new, free air
the slow red
the neck's sudden angle.

Nothing is rare about this morning
but what I make of it: give
the sickened tree another landhold
where the dying branch is
sawed and burned—
a cure that will not last
yet how can loss be transmuted
if not faithfully accrued?

Unshaded, the house will not outlive me.
There is cycle, and a change in
how much cloud covers.
In the grave cloths of the sky
I prepare for your firmament.

THE BOY AND THE CATCH

When you put your head down, wearing the face
of water, ear
missing by no more than fool
the fish's mouth, what did you hear?

It was no bad match: seven years of boy
and now, near an even
seven pounds of fish lie in
your pail—we watched the weighing.

And yet no contest: hooks are not designed
to slide out; we can bear
only so much risk, and hearts
will snarl on the killing art.

So this one stalled your heart by just living
enough. Dying's easy:
we carry the knives. Only,
a god had whispered, "Help me!"

HURRICANE OVER A COUNTRY BORDERING ON THE GULF OF MEXICO

Under the Crab
wind rising
a priest
sings
malignitas tutissima cassis
evil to all in this house:

out of the astrologers
rain like mountains
we can neither plow
nor prophesy
there are no walls
the cenotaphs are crumbling

the wind is vulture
tearing our hands
from the stars

we have buried our fathers
there are no more mouths
to cry.

TWO WINDOWS OF THE CATHEDRAL

   1. *Crucifixion*

Mary, they have led you
where the wind is indiscreet. They have
taken away the robe.

Mary, your hair spins
like the flags of their lances.
The air grows stiff
and a blade partitions your innocent life.

Tell them you were symbol not sacrifice.
They are the ones who have cut wood
for the branched thing where the nails are struck
until you cry, "Stop! I will
give it to you for nothing."

Mary, who are the fools? Why do you
believe and believe? Is there a hand down
from the sky, up from a cracked pod
of earth, summoning you?

Mary, let them take someone else.
Make them hang
the clothes on the vagrant bones again.
This is your window.

2. *Ste. Jeanne*

After the last rape
they set you on your pile of sticks
careful as though, like the Dauphine's doll
a glass face could break.

Legs that strode you to Reims
suddenly stuffed with dead leaves
when the square came into view
are muscled now
by the ropes that roll up your thighs.
In the end, this stake is home.

When fire mounts like a harvest
your eyes — over the crowning grain —
meet his. Chaste jailer
who took you here.
Is this love immolating a boy
and a girl? Somewhere
perhaps in Domremy — ah,
if he had come sooner!

The twigs thrust in by a priest
you confessed to ages ago
minutes ago
cross in your hands
will have a quicker death.
Woman, as your breath smokes
as the child melts from your womb
the brands on your breast
are our tongues.

MONET'S GARDEN: IN CAMERA

North of the Seine, what country was it: light
without amnesty, white hands of the cliffs
tempera of flood plain earth.
And always the garden: the garden.

Hands playing
the alluvial
music in camera logic:
a willow as tree
nothing more.
It stoops to the pond:
leaf-fall
on lilies
on reeds
that surface
from the quickening
mud, water
dying.
An artist poled his boat:
moot
in litter
of the drowned
and the risen.
A rake
that would be
an easel
across his arm.
And the camera sees:

for that mitered second
comes upon a heaven of color
then closes. So inhuman dark flows over his
dredged world. This is what the blind already know.

THE LAST SUMMER IN LLANBERIS

1.

In the north of Wales.
I bend to its weather
for the last time.
Rivers tense
at the dismembered feet
of castles
and Snowden stands, cloud-blind.

This morning
rain shreds the road, streams
scour the patriarchal glens.
One is ragged
by the fiction of fire
at the heart.

2.

In my country, a boy
has died:
his wheels like querns, milling
the grainless air.
A wall whored him, and each
hard bone's kernel
rushed open.

This year
a seedless light falls.
There are fissures
in the freighted news.
A door shuts
on a room still hot with life:
the out-closing
of love.
Oh, the blood will not wash.

3.

In a sky that resolves to divisible pain
the geese fly south on safe
ordinary missions.
And where I strain to see them
the day lets in only
what one can take from its hands.

By late season: the birds finished
rain gone
the rivers quiet, again
and a colder sun sweeping the wall.

ORNITHOLOGY IN NOVEMBER

Rain coats the brown slab of a field.
The cropped corn stalks
and the kernels, left behind
by the silage-makers
are a bread line
for birds in the uncertain economies
of migration.
Whimbrels, doves, red finches
and the ubiquitous geese
spreading from Canada
are a farm's new yield.
Turnstones try the knots of earth
which will do instead of rocks
to spin and lay open
the sleeping grubs.
Nervous, their wings worn thin
before what storms
now the flocks come as inmates
from a nesting ark
released together; landing
like raw dancers. And as we are
audience, we sweeten
with the dung spread across their stage.

It is the grace of celebration
— of recreation — and the redemption
of gifts from the dead plain.

Without such seasoning, the birds
understand nothing
will return in spring
not blood roses that smear
the next scene red

not another stand of corn
not the north-flying plovers
whose mating plumage ripens
like the seeds of winter wheat.
They know that, without knowing how
each act matters to the others.
We know this dependence comes
like the treaties
of a long and deciduous marriage.

CHRISTMAS BIRD COUNT

Our windows open to a field
planted with birds.
Like all crops
this one needs tending.

You read the signs
paint words with guano: soon
it will snow
making all rules the same.

And when it is over
when there is nothing that is
not white or black
about us
the time will be, to draw a line
around the figures.

In other months
some singing begins.

II

HOMECOMING OF THE NORTH COAST WIFE

for
Mary Johnston Marsh
Mary Marsh Wilson and
Edith Mary Wilson Phillips

*"The leaves have fallen
and they are not last
autumn's leaves."*
—Viktor Shklovsky

FARM WIFE AT HARVEST

When you draw the blade's road through grain
it is not to earn a new womanshape.
That dream turned in the first parturition.
Now the furrows of your eyes are patient:
have learned to hold their lines.
This harvest will come
because
whatever the field bares
you will walk in a cleared farm
the strong conquered rows at your feet
as if, at last, some things move ahead:
what you are, and I will hear of.
You will not spare the sequences of reaping
and age.
These will come into your hands
like warring but faithful lovers.

HER TOPOGRAPHY

The blue fruits of the juniper are ripe,
a blue vase hangs in the window, and a wren calls
to it from the tree: "Piper. Piper. Pipe."

The bird spins its voice: webbing the squalls
of unsettled weather. The vase holds a leaf
turning white. Piper, pipe green walls

for it and halls floored green as green's grief:
the year at death. But the berries love
their own skins, and a song is love, briefly.

How the leaf wants sun-love when there's no sun, but cuffs
of rain ringing its glass like birdsong
in minor. Cold. And her hands are skeletons in gloves.

The rain paints a life, stripe after long
stripe. Surreal. The white leaf. The blue falls
on evergreen. The wren. The bones shielded from belief.
They are her Sierras. Asia or Africa. The home stuff.

WHERE THE BARN LEANS EMPTY

And says our farewell word...
— John Logan

A dying woodlot
meets the year's spring sheep.
Leaves torn at the edge of winter
rake across their fleece
and will not stay.
The fragile business is still undone.

One more act lies ahead: for me
an opposite birth.
It is what the barn learns, only
now tilting
a little in that direction.
It is what astonished lambs will come to.

The failing trees mirror themselves:
no face retrievable.
Skin, the reflection of a deeper glass.

On the way
one stick is companion:
the walking branch that balances
my track and wears the earth
like an erosion.
I'm familiar and not far from home.

So. Indigent wood, the flock
this quiet storehouse are company
in the sweet mud that haunts my feet.
What public shape is given them?
What poem's written on me?
By what graves' names are we called?

HOMECOMING OF THE NORTH COAST WIFE

The rain stumbles without notice
to a closure.

For a while, leaves will be sluices
unsteady drains

the downward cast
eyes have, as a season moves on.

Now you and I
or two who have been intimate

walk these hard won fields, each footstep
like an earth nail.

The rain is salt.
I think of Lot's wife: her sour ground.

THE DAY COLOR WARPED
FROM OUR SISTER'S EYES

First the ring around the lamp
then nothing where your shoulders were.
Notebooks on doctors' shelves
shadows around the words.
Your white nails.

The world has always been too much
a pattern of grays
since you've known it
even when sun clayed the dawn
and green was a rag of April.
Is it time
for only one outer and one inner sight?

Your eyes are plums, furred
as the fruit
hard with the juices
but will not ripen again.

Sister, it is too soon.
They haven't invented a cure.
From now on
we will have
the moss of your voice
on our north side
and from the sea, pearls
shaken out of the oyster
that is your pain.

A DISCRETE FLOWERING

Beating the rain home
when the sky is a dying man filled with pain
I am the caretaker
who stops where first drops roll
off the garden: its sweat
like a face mask.

The cold man sleeps in his house
bones growing light
as light bends
around his next corner.

A woman can do more
than bring in the August weeds
but knows that death will be a discrete
flowering, knows
there is not comfort, only compassion.

Rain is today's wage buried
in my skin; no
difference now between
the life before and this storm.
I pull a bud from its cloister.
My father opens
into the rocks, the soil, the roots.

FIRST SON

Valedictory.
The word strikes off the page
as today's rain leaps
from the trees' arms
to mine
hanging empty
beside a grave I haven't seen.
Your stone is planted.
If we are of the same earth
it is wet:
running
with the sweet, cold sound
of your name
ungiven, so
unforgotten....
This is an old bearing
down
for the living children
who followed
you
an old, heavy soil
in which you stir like
the insects
and the animals you feed.
It is *welcome* long
coming
as a storm:
as the stream's hard song to its bed
as the rain that takes the shape
of the other word.

THE CHRISTENING OF THE MONGOLOID CHILD

Cold bird fly
into the shadow of the sun, fly mad
into his mouth. Your seed
cracks light like the beak of heaven.

Stars black
as the color my pillow wears
black as wings
in his eyes: where you die there
bird, I will eat your cries.

WHEN THEY PULL YOU FROM MY RIVER, CAROLING

at light and the sacred walls
I say, "She is not my child
let me sleep."
When I open my eyes again
you have determined to stay:
to take the apple whole.

Your fist fits in my mouth
I smell your new skin
as if it were still mine.

Once, in the birthing hut
I grunted over a hole
lined with fur and sweat.
Later ropes, warped to the bed's mooring,
bore out the storm.
Now, air, swallowed with each pain,
smokes like an innocent fire
the day your face turns to me.

When you and I are done with this
when it is more than a beginning and we can
walk through the morning
daughter
there will yet be
some staking out of the dark.

THE CARETAKERS:
CLOSING FOR A SEASON

We have locked the glass
doors around your house, leaving
a museum—an exhibition
of finished things
and the untried flotsam.
Flowers in your garden—
sun's clutch
in the curfew of our hands.
The breeze smells of wild grape
the path to the cove
grows over.
For the insects, these
fields are *las corridas*.
How you miss them!
Miss the straight hornet thrust
the dying cicada's *Ole!*

There is no heat
in this summer's home.
Stay—
and winter poles
its raft into the bones.
The bugs and blossoms freeze.
In the cold, we
whose turn comes
draw close to them, touch
their stiff auroras
cradle ourselves in the seamless
arms—and praise.
Listen.
The sword is passed
to you, for, *Ole! Ole!* we die.

THREE POEMS AT THE FALL EQUINOX

This gathering for the cold
is a reversal, yet
the world flares:
small black and white birds
calling at feeders;
evergreens' quills
that punctuate the paper soil.
Where a pond is filled
or emptied by sea
the tide reels or casts the changes
that disclose themselves.

    *

So. A girl (who was blind?) cries
over the garden, comforting new
graves.
What comes will
slide down ridges of winter
like the nomad ice:
her hands in the snow
in your hair.

    *

There is flame enough
but a storm child lives here, still.
You know how logs burn, and
tend fire, while
that one
who fishes off the channel bridge
sees her sister's face
swimming in the shifts below.

OVER DARTMOOR: THE CLIMB AT HOUND TOR

Up here
the wind is
a dog hungry
for the shape of a bone.
Below the rock where I reign
bracken, dead
for the year, spreads
brown ribs
restless as clocks.

I have ticked up these hills
waiting
for the clock in my breast to strike
for the dog's teeth in my side
to leave me
the hole.

He cries off
at last
answering you
and the thing he drops
at your feet, mastering
this naked place, is
like the blade of a dull knife.

You pick it up.

I watch you climb, grow
life-sized around cracks and hard places
of the mountain to stand
beside me
under the wind
stuffing my rib into your high left pocket.

J. CALVIN'S DAUGHTER

*We are all haunted, even at
third or fourth hand....it's
a little cruel— but harder,
better."* —Thomas Williams

Now the snow is deep where, long-shanked,
dogs prowl the salable woods.
I look to them
from a window: this woman
indebted to glass.

To the dogs
the day is what it is.
Real, because all they have
faces them:
a skunk sprays
a bird freezes and falls
shadows become
squirrels in their winter heat.
And these hounds answer
home, called
by a witness who has rattled the air
around them
since they were born.

I owe them
the freedom of these woods.
What if a day churns
in the wind and mercury cracks
its glass
in the snow's fire?
If I stand before the thicker pain
of a blizzard taking the world
this, too, is owing.

MOTION COUNTERCLOCKWISE

This is a patient snow
tenable
a waiter not so quick
to go as come.

Not young, wrinkled
it wears
the marks of our feet
as growth rings
signs of aging and a neat cunning
in arithmetic.

Like us, the snow
will live a while longer
its bones thinner
below the surface
yet will not
let on that the pain spreads.

Inside it is dark
each day diminishes.

Write
justice.
There is law
snow can
not hide:

GROUND-HOG DAY

To stand is to discover how
your heart races in the cold
rooms of a holed-up winter
the sun, still tunneled in clouds
and you, close inside the fur

that is your skin: there is nothing
to do about the alleys below your garden
but wait for the woodchuck to come out.
Something held under what the others see.
Warm and slow, it sleeps half the year
then puts its nose up, sniffs, chews
a stick, makes a small noise in its throat
goes back into the hole while
the forecasters ask:
Did you see her? Shadow

and dreams are what you return to.
Even the unlicensed belong. In here
there is accrual
the way a winter leaf grows: so
quiet there's no telling how it will turn bold
entering the savage corridors of spring.

TO A HOUSE ON THE MARKET

It is a sane place, the ground lies as if
assigned and willing: down
well and smooth, though I have found
it cranky with moles or crowds

of ants worked under the skin. I have watched
trees, there, go from black to green.
The way widows drop mourning
veils. I say it imagines

seasons: one where a part dies, others when
candles finger the pines
or lightning is a rawhide
rope in the hands of rain.

The house stains me as if it were a friend
painted out of my life, yet
about whom I still sing:
as a woman going old lifts

her head and hears, and hears.

III

FALLING INTO THE DREAM

for
the Children

"What is love?
One name for it is knowledge."
— Robert Penn Warren

SUMMER ISLAND

There was a light about
the mornings
as if the sun had never notched us
before:
as if its hills stirred a color
no one had worn
until now.
An island is that way
sprouting on the horizon
like corn:
green shocks
in the last thick month
of summer.
Our places choose us
and those days, coming back
bright as new metal,
there was a kind of belling
as if we were harnessed to a steeple
and this place:
the old man on the rope.

IN THE MID-ISLAND

This is where the world begins
and ends:
the elms that die
slowly, the young men
in clay-cuffed levis
talking of the summer
the rainless mornings
the dry fields, the women
who wait table on the State Road
and bring home the tips;
come home
to naked beds in kerosene light
and, after making love
go out to the two-machine laundromat
behind the trees
while their men shine
'74 pickups at a do-it-yourself carwash.

Nights after
the store closes
and the post office under the same roof
tourists will come
to Daddy's Forge Restaurant.
They will eat cranberry cake
and wild blueberry ice
while the women circle their tables
serving coffee in glass cups, remembering
money will be harder to come by
past Labor Day.

It will rain
between then and now
the corn will come in
sheep will be brought back
from the salt marsh meadows, bloated
will crop our grass
not so high since June
while the elm bark beetles get
their old playmates ready.

I have told you these things
because they are what you would learn to know
in the summer here.
As for the winter
it is long
as a woman's term.

EXHIBITION IN RAIN

The weather leaves this meadow
open; enter it, wearing
your new clothes:
the red hat
the blue slicker.
Drops nest in hair
on your hands' spring skin.
In this gallery
the green sculptures add their color
where none was but your own.

Judging, you test
the immersive crafts: sepals
and capsules are tongues, throats
and the vagrant arms;
from archetypal stems see
now churched spires, masts, javelins.
Earth, the base metal in which they stand
is hammered, and severed, and whole.

As you go, there are prizes
to leave for the beautiful: touching
the winners, you say
Dragon's Mouth
Carrion Flower, Bloodroot, Adam and Eve.

APRIL FOOL'S DAY

A day like this:
the grass implacable
a robin's ears ringing
to the clappers of the wind, clouds
hungering at
the windows like trolls.
And the water of the ponds:
yesterday, flat sheet metal skins
today
camelbacks.
In such change we are lovers
each of whom has not read
the other
and the song in a bird's heart
is one
it does not understand
yet obeys.

BEACHCOMBING IN SKEIN COVE

This half-ocean's heart is accountable
in miles from headland
to headland:
a treasure hunt like sleep
I measure
and will pay out from end to end.

The sea falls
from a corner of the god's eye
a last gull call is withheld
sheep balance on the horizon.
I have become a log:
the jetsam that floats at his feet
unwilling yet willed.
Or the hand.

Each day is only-begotten
and the world whole.
I have begun the naming.

NOTES FOR SWIMMING OR DANCING AFTER A LUNAR ECLIPSE

The whetstone of shadow
against moon.
Lust, beautiful in the dark
stations of love.
The pale, trusting song
that sinks at dawn.

And morning is a nocturne
an ocean scored
by the star in its throat.
We swim here
one stroke at a time
conjure only
what we know how to do
in the half-day.
Look
I tell you
this
this is the old music.
It is the difference
the dance
between want and need.

FLOCKING

This tribe has been over-wrought for days;
crabby, jangling the bells of the air
wild as warped clappers to ring away

clean; hard not to go when the blood is on;
hard not to know why your wings only shift
from tree to tree, while you kick at the sun

rafted in hot grass. How do
you take the sky on? It's no easy touch.
Robins are too ready, won't wait while dew

thickens; just wise enough to know
leaving's quick, or you'll grow graves of wings.
I read white circles of their eyes like snow.

They will out-fly me, will holler up winter,
cry rings around my slower wind.
It isn't every day that sows this kind of hunger.

The air from now to stop is a million wing-
beats long. I can't tell, maybe the best go.
There's always dying here—
some of us will make it to spring.

WHEN THE SEA BIRD HAS GONE: CONCERT

The plainsong of a heron
wakes us: mornings
at the sand's lip.
And the tide backs off
taking the bird beyond sound.
It is one day nearer
the end of a season
as each day is now.
This flier will follow a sea
that leads his shad, his herring
further and further south.
While you and I and
some others stay behind
in the caesura between
old and new.
On a coast that is scored
for absent voices
we listen to the ones who remain:
crows and the drought wind.
Their hard, faultless music.

POEM FOR THE SUMMER

Snow falls across the sun.
A woman on the porch chases crows
to make room
for chickadees
and the rachet-voiced jays.

The northwest wind
this season wipes her table-
land clean even
of the eager birds
and this slow white yeast
that rises
with the dead of the year.

Behind her, beyond window
ice, the heat
of jazz and Mendelssohn.
And in one cool room
words whine like a real wind.

This home is seed and leaf:
a poem
blown onto the page
the star
blind but stumbling closer.

LETTERS FROM THE ISLANDS

1. *To H.H. in Skye*

So your life is to fish — just —
in those reeling streams? I have
learned the myths of what swims in
the black water: we live with
them in this other place. And
our creek, stained from oak not peat
sluices fright-molting ducks. Once
my son took a small-mouthed bass
in the pool; he hasn't cast
since. I believe not out of love.
Fear, perhaps. Yes. I am afraid
of how much game eludes us.

2. *from Madeira*

Only Islas Desertas off-shore:
the trap is real, a thick bread on
your table, drought in the old alleyways.
In May, the jacaranda flowers
but all this year on the Avenida
do Mar, fumes are the evil in town.
Seven hundred miles from Portugal
with no absolution from the wind
you live volcanically, drive tourists
to the calderada, stare outlawed
across the ocean where nothing, not even
a stray bird, relives the memory of
escape. You have come to paradise.

3. *Moving to the Caribbean*

Imagine the sea itself, stretched
as a cat stretches, full-length:
its green transparent, its base
yellow sun on yellow sand.
Think of easing into the sea.
Think of people, beautiful
but happy; think of them not
beautiful but happy.
This move could take us beyond
the islands, to South America:
Brazil. In our time we could
hold flight by the hand. The wind
fills our arms, our mouths with salt.
Our kisses: doors always keyed
to quick hot rain. The sky wrapped
around us clearing until
the next endurable storm.

4. *This*

We can live anywhere.
Now, air, swallowed with each pain,
smokes like an innocent fire
the day your face turns to me.

When you and I are done with this
when it is more than a beginning and we can
walk through the morning
daughter
there will yet be
some staking out of the dark.

SEA FIRE

On this island of the mourning
hills, long clouds lick—like the roving
tongues of women in their black-walled
huts. Beds hard and sweet. The men hauled
rough and tender from the loving
hellbent sea. Above, there's fracture
where the thick rocks wheel; a spoiling
wind lets down, as though the gods crawled
                on this island.

The steep bays are theirs: closures
come like blind girls, fingers tuning
light from harps—music the peat held.
And what flares we call sea fire, cold
but home. The madness we go in
                on this island.

WRITING THE OCEAN AFTER A STORM

The lamps have died.
Tonight wheels rumble, coaching the hill:
a sound more solid than the leaves
of unreconciled air.
After the rain, no birds knock
mice struggle in their sleep
and the clothes lie
piled—arms and legs across
the in-folded bodies—blind
among the inconsequence of lavender
and bay.
Over our thin beds
salt and damp, no star chimes.
A caravan rings the house
wagons hissing in the sand-fed grass.
here, as the silence grows less in us
the sea shoulders our names
and the rest
that we touch and are afraid to touch.

OCTOBER

Because she is still unweaned
the girl leaves home.
A bitch comes
into season; cattle are at their fattening
in the fields' thick rooms.
And ducks—the mallards, pintails, teal—
are resonant in ponds.

It is what happens this month:
the opening on the other side of a tree
the slow turning
as if one and every compass sweeps
from north to south.

Days begin their dark
quickly
where sun relinquishes the earth.
A catbird's nest
is empty
in the wild wrinkled rose.

Air is silent:
an epilogue rises.

It is memory: the home suspended.

Somewhere the world breaks.
Many grieve.

Alone, and far
among them
a woman echoes in the bleeding child.

TWO WHO DIED BEFORE WINTER

(for E.W.P. and C.W.P.)

They anchor to the truths
of their graves.
Float
in bodies feral
as the wind of their mute hearts.
In the end I
have learned what it is
to take leave:
a valley where water lies
like a stricken coin, scarred
and signed
and irreplaceable.

FALLING INTO THE DREAM

The snow isn't thick
when you enter the trees
a book in your pocket
to help with the birds
that will ramble overhead.
Nor is the cold intense.
In the underbrush
something dark strokes the ground:
this season a cat hunts
as her sisters sleep
in the nest, and because of it
the woods are still.
Except that a jay screams once
when two shadows pass.

In here, there's a knot of hope
and fear
like an unobstructed sun.
The snow isn't thick
and your shoes are quiet
among the winter weeds.
There is no path.
This time you don't ask
where am I
going, where am I going?

FLOOD:
THE ISLAND BECOMES WATER

The wool of this place is shorn
and a weather watch begins
on Noah's Hill.
There is an edge moving closer
over which we are to fall.

You say the land is high
pitched like a good builder's roof.
I say this thing coming is the Siamese half.

We calculate its crawl
through hollows in the sand, the time
to fill gullies and gardens
to dock at the foot of the final ridge.

As water, the island will drive its wedge
between us; as we wait, you and I
account for the halves of scrupulous lives.

THE HOUSE OF RECEIVING

The Gift

Sun honors the dust as gold
after the lineal rain.
In the house
a room is chosen to filter
the bullion through—
a bowl
when, as clouds return
it is stored for someone
who will put in her hands to stir
the light
but will not steal it.

Age

Where the land is, there will be
ocean in 4,000 years—
its sediment holding her fossil
whose print is the vein
building
a new mother lode.

But today this woman walks
the tenacious edge
counting
the little stones that were whales' ribs
sharks' teeth, counting
the fungi she calls earth stars.
There are more like these
at home
where the scavenging collects.

She is of those whose blood slows
who foretell
the barrenness of each coast
and require an accounting for each
seedless month.

The Death

The lining of home
pads her year's floor, as winter
returns winter.
It is a grass shaded
to match
the brittle fur of a mole
the woman has found unburied.
When there is rain now
when the ground pours
tunnels
open like the runs in a cloth
that has spent its youth.
And the frayed water
washes
this small enemy
into her hand.

NAMING THE ISLAND

1.

No relief to the sea
in the months of wind.
Sun is hallucination, the sky
only clears at night.
We face each other
over tables, changeless
as the dull spray
that is pain
or grief
until neither pain nor grief
instruct.

2.

Spring hauls south to north
shoots from the quivers of ponds
plays the grass
like cool strings: love
sprawls
new-leaved on the fresh
and dying dunes.

We come out of a bad dream
go on our knees
to the old paintmakers' stones
invoke the god whose foot this island is:
naming it for his legend
for a Viking
for a queen
naming it the affordable names
we give ourselves.

THE WARMING OF A GLASS HOUSE

(for R.H.N.)

It is the first brittle morning.
A web of ice rules
the frail syntax of windowpanes
    like some permanent unions
       that nevertheless dissolve and meet
       again, new.
Cold outside, warmer in.
The fire is lit.

This house has sequential heat:
a stove for the horded
nucleal wood:
    then you, split by therms
    of sleep and wake, coming
    down the stairs.